PUFFIN  LITTLE

Little
Explorer

PUFFIN BOOKS

UK | USA | Canada | Ireland | Australia
India | New Zealand | South Africa | China

Penguin Random House Australia is part of the Penguin Random House group of companies
whose addresses can be found at global.penguinrandomhouse.com.

First published by Puffin Books, an imprint of Penguin Random House Australia Pty Ltd, in 2020

Printed in China

A catalogue record for this
book is available from the
National Library of Australia

ISBN 978 1 76 089766 6

Penguin Random House Australia uses papers that are natural and recyclable products,
made from wood grown in sustainable forests. The logging and manufacture processes are
expected to conform to the environmental regulations of the country of origin.

penguin.com.au

The Ocean

PUFFIN BOOKS

HELLO, LITTLE EXPLORERS

WELCOME TO THE OCEAN...

There's a big underwater adventure in store for us.

I can't wait to see what we discover in the **OCEAN** together!

There's nowhere on Earth that's quite as mysterious as the ocean. It's such an exciting place for us to dive into!

The ocean has lots of new and interesting things for Little Explorers to discover – from its shallows all the way to its depths.

We might be LITTLE, but we've got some **BIG** facts to learn.

Are you ready?

Then turn the page . . .

WHAT IS THE OCEAN?

The **ocean** is what we call the **water** that fills the space between Earth's **continents**. It covers more than two thirds of our planet's surface and holds almost all of our water.

BENEATH THE WAVES

The water in our oceans is salty and full of **life**. In fact, the majority of the plants and animals on our planet live in the ocean!

This is what makes the ocean so exciting for Little Explorers to visit.

From tiny creatures like **plankton** to schools of **fish** and giant **blue whales** – as well as marine plants like **kelp** and **seaweed** – there's so much for us to discover. I hope you've brought your flippers!

The mix of plants and animals in the ocean keeps it healthy, because all this life is connected in a **food web**. A food web is made up of a complex system of food chains.

BIODIVERSITY

A food web thrives when it has a wide variety of plants and animals. This diversity supports lots of different life forms up and down the food chain.

This is called **biodiversity.** It refers to the many different life forms that can be found on Earth, and the connections between them in the food web. From tiny **microorganisms** and **plants**, to **fungi** and **animals**; everything is interconnected, including the environments that they call home.

Biodiversity is what makes our planet so very special.

There are lots of other interesting things in the ocean that aren't alive.

Did you know the ocean has some of the tallest **mountains** on Earth, is home to underwater **volcanoes** and is the part of our planet's surface that is closest to Earth's central core?

There's so much to discover!

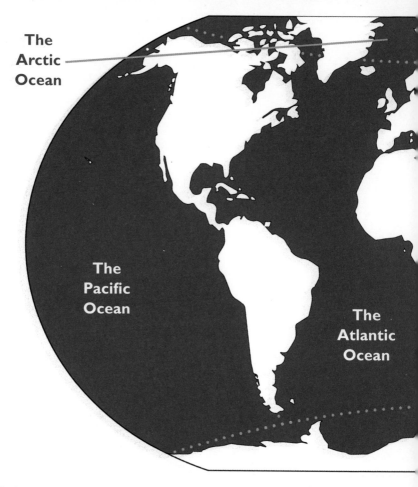

The Arctic Ocean

The Pacific Ocean

The Atlantic Ocean

There are five oceans on our planet.

The Pacific Ocean is our biggest – and deepest – ocean.

The Atlantic Ocean is home to the world's richest fishing grounds.

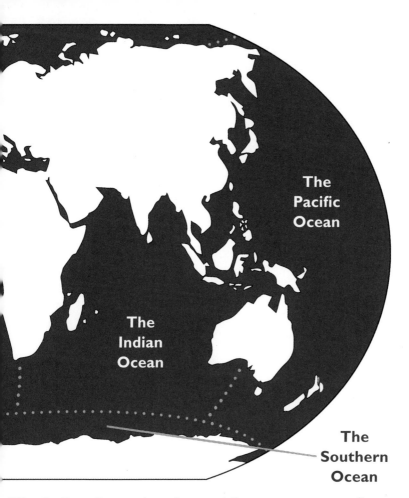

The Pacific Ocean

The Indian Ocean

The Southern Ocean

The Indian Ocean has the world's youngest ocean floor.

The Southern Ocean is the ocean around Antarctica.

The Arctic Ocean is Earth's smallest ocean, and it is also the shallowest.

WHAT IS A SEA?

Seas are usually **smaller** and **shallower** than oceans. The word 'sea' tends to refer to areas of saltwater that are at least partially surrounded by land.

There are a **lot** of seas on our planet. Some are quite large, like the Mediterranean Sea, and some are not connected to the ocean at all, like the Dead Sea, which is actually just a very large lake!

The Dead Sea isn't deadly, but its water is so salty that no creatures can live there!

BIRDS OF THE SEA

Not all sea life lives under the waves. There are many **seabirds** that spend much of their lives out on the ocean, and many more that make their homes along our coastlines and on islands. They feed on fish and other small animals that live in the ocean.

One of these birds is me, the **PUFFIN!** Like many seabirds, puffins hunt by diving underwater to catch fish. Yummy!

Seabirds come in all shapes and sizes – from giant **albatrosses** to tiny **petrels**, and from awkward **penguins** to graceful **eagles**.

The first stop on our ocean exploration is the shallow areas that make up our **COASTAL WATERS** – where the ocean meets the land.

This is where most of us interact with the ocean, and where Little Explorers can see so many amazing things.

All oceans have places where the water meets the land, and these places vary across the world, from coast to coast.

When you're exploring coastal waters, you could be:

- examining a **rock pool**
- swimming at a **beach**
- grazing with manatees in a **seagrass meadow**
- playing with seals in **kelp forests**
- snorkelling over a **coral reef**

These all describe different types of coastal **ecosystems**.

An ecosystem is a community of different plants and animals living together in a certain environment.

Even though our coastal waters have many different ecosystems, there are some things they have in common: each coastal environment has shallow water and lots and lots of life!

ROCK POOLS

These puddles of water are created in the **cracks** and **crevices** of coastline rocks when the tide goes out. The tide is the rise and fall of the ocean caused by the gravitational pull of the sun and moon.

Little Explorers can find fish and crabs in rock pools. Some creatures, like fish, come and go with each tide. Others, like anemones and crabs, make rock pools their home!

Rock pools can be very harsh environments, with some constantly battered by waves. Despite this, they contain entire communities of little ocean creatures.

It's very important to try not to disturb rock pools while we observe what lives inside them.

Rock pool ecosystems are filled with soft, colourful **anemones** and spiky **sea urchins** – which look like plants but are actually animals.

They are also home to many other animals, including squishy **sea cucumbers** and creatures like **starfish**, which are not really fish at all!

There *are* some fish in rock pools though, living in tiny schools that flit in and out of cover.

Little Explorers can often see **crabs** scuttling about on the rocks too, and some pools might even be home to an **octopus!**

BEACHES

Beaches are made up of rocks, shells and bones that have been ground down by waves or the wind. Observant Little Explorers can find clues about the animals that live in the deeper ocean by taking a close look at the things that wash up on our beaches.

Have you ever seen a **cuttlebone** when walking along the sand? Cuttlebones are white, oval shells that come from cuttlefish. We can also often see shells that were once part of an animal like a **clam**, and lots and lots of **seaweed**.

It can be tempting to collect the things that wash up on the shore, but if we do this, we're taking away important parts of the ecosystem that animals rely on for food and shelter.

Many animals live in the waters around beaches. Schools of fish like **flathead** and **snapper** swim beneath the waves, along with bigger fish like **great white sharks** and **tiger sharks**.

Next time you visit the beach, you could keep an eye out for mammals like **seals, whales** and even **penguins** too.

Waves are fun for humans to play in, but there's an ocean animal that likes to play in the surf as well – the **dolphin!**

Dolphins are very smart, and work together in pods to hunt fish, squid and other ocean animals. There are many different species of dolphin. Some, like the **bottlenose dolphin**, are common, but others like the **humpback dolphin** are endangered. This means there aren't many of them left.

SEAGRASS MEADOWS

Seagrass meadows are huge plains of seagrass that grow under just a few metres of water because, like grass on land, it needs sunlight to grow. The shallow ocean around Western Australia has some of the biggest seagrass meadows on Earth!

Dugongs – also called sea cows – graze on the seagrass that grow in these meadows. Dugongs look like a cross between a dolphin and a hippopotamus, and they can grow to be almost 3 metres long!

Little Explorers can also find graceful **eagle rays**, soft **sea slugs**, slow-moving **turtles** and more among the grass.

Seagrass meadows are very important in coastal areas. The roots of the grass hold the sandy ocean floor in place, so that the waves don't wash it away.

The grass also filters the water so that all the marine animals that live in and around it stay healthy.

Seagrass meadows also absorb and store a lot of **carbon dioxide**. In fact, they're better at doing this than almost any other environment in the world.

Reducing the amount of carbon dioxide in the atmosphere is important, because it helps to combat the effects of **climate change**. This makes sure that *all* of the ecosystems on our planet can survive.

KELP FORESTS

Kelp is a kind of seaweed that grows very tall, very quickly – some types grow up to 60 centimetres a day. It grows in cold, shallow water, and can reach more than 40 metres in height!

Around one quarter of Earth's coastlines are **kelp forests**, which are home to many different types of **rockfish**, **crabs** and **snails**.

Here, Little Explorers can find animals like **seahorses** and **sea dragons** holding onto the kelp with their tails. Sea dragons look particularly leafy, and blend right in to the kelp. Though they don't look like it, both of these creatures are actually types of fish!

Seals and **sea lions** use kelp forests as shelter, hiding from sharks among the tall fronds. They hunt the fish that live there, and they also love to play!

Sea urchins live in kelp forests too, and feast on the kelp fronds. Thankfully, other forms of sea life like **fish, crabs, eels** and **sea otters** feed on the urchins, making sure these spiky creatures don't eat *all* the kelp. The many animals that live in the kelp forest work together to keep their home healthy.

Everything in an ecosystem works together to make sure that the balance of life is preserved.

CORAL REEFS

Okay, Little Explorers, let's leave the cool coastal waters we've explored so far and head somewhere **warmer**. Don't forget your sunscreen!

Coral reefs are one of our most unique ecosystems, and they are some of the largest living structures on the planet. They also live for thousands of years, making them Earth's oldest living animals.

That's right, coral is an **animal**, not a plant! In fact, what we think of as a coral isn't even *one* animal. A single branch or head of coral is actually made up of an entire colony of little creatures called **polyps**.

There are two different kinds of coral. **Hard corals,** like brain and staghorn coral, and **soft corals,** like sea fans. Corals come in many different colours, creating an underwater kaleidoscope for Little Explorers to enjoy.

As our climate changes, though, so does the ocean. When the water around a reef gets *too* warm, something called **coral bleaching** happens, altering the health of the entire ecosystem.

There are **many, many, many** animals that live in coral-reef ecosystems – so many that Big Explorers are discovering new species all the time!

Lots of the fish species that live in coral reefs can't survive in any other marine ecosystem.

Because healthy coral is so colourful, lots of the fish that live in a coral reef are brightly coloured so they can blend in.

Some fish, like **clownfish** and **damselfish**, are only a handful of colours. But some fish, like **parrot fish**, have an entire rainbow on their scales!

The fish in coral ecosystems also come in all different sizes, from **redeye gobies** that are only a couple of centimetres long to **groupers** that can grow up to two and a half metres!

Coral reefs are home to many different species of **sharks** and **turtles**, and the warm waters that surround them are nurseries for whales and their babies.

Coral reefs truly are teeming with life!

MARINE RESERVES

The coastal waters of our oceans are easily accessible to Big and Little Explorers, which means it's easy for us to accidentally cause them harm. To make sure we keep these ecosystems safe, many parts of our coastlines and shallow waters have been made into **marine reserves** or parks.

This means that certain things we are allowed to do in these areas, like boating and fishing, are limited, which makes sure that the plants and animals that live there can thrive.

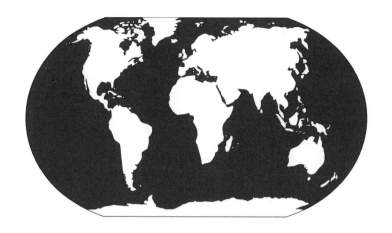

We've already learnt that **biodiversity** – a wide variety of plants and animals – is important for life all over the world. We've also discovered that the plants in the ocean help to keep our climate stable. Having marine parks helps protect our entire planet from harm.

The **OPEN OCEAN** is the huge expanse of water between the coastal shallows and the deep ocean. It's home to all sorts of wonderful things. Let's go take a look!

Despite being so big, the open ocean is home to only one tenth of our marine wildlife. But that doesn't mean there's not lots to explore – the open ocean is the largest wilderness on Earth, after all. So come with me, Little Explorers, and let's dive down!

The ocean is an average of 4 kilometres deep, but some parts dip far deeper. If you were to walk that far on land, it would take you a whole hour! Because the ocean is so deep, life occurs in different layers, which Big Explorers have named by the amount of light they receive.

The top layer of water is called the **sunlight zone**, because it receives a lot of sunlight.

The middle layer of water is called the **twilight zone**. Reaching from 200 metres to 1000 metres underwater, this layer only receives a little sun.

The deepest layer of water stretches all the way to the ocean floor, and it receives no light at all. This is called the **midnight zone**.

Let's find out more about the open ocean. Follow me!

WHALES

Most of the marine life that Big Explorers have discovered lives in the **sunlight zone**. It's not only easier to explore the ocean's surface than it is to reach deeper waters, but this is where ocean animals find most of their food.

The food web of the open ocean starts with a very small but very important food source – **plankton**.

Whales that eat plankton are called **baleen whales**, and they have a filter called baleen in their mouth that acts as a sieve. To eat, these whales take giant gulps of water and then push it back out through their baleen, trapping the plankton inside.

The **blue whale**, the world's largest mammal, is a baleen whale and so is the **bowhead whale**, the world's longest-living mammal, with a lifespan of 200 years!

WHAT ARE PLANKTON?

Plankton are sea creatures that are carried from place to place by ocean currents.

They can be teeny tiny plants and animals or larger creatures like krill and jellyfish – and they are a whale's favourite snack!

FISH

Fish eat plankton too. Countless fish live in the open ocean in groups called schools. The biggest schools can be made up of over **one billion** fish!

Living in a school helps to protect individual fish from being eaten by larger predatory fish and mammals.

Fish come in all shapes and sizes. When **pufferfish** are threatened, they can double their size and make themselves spiky. **Oarfish** are long and skinny like a snake.

Some of the strangest-looking fish in the ocean are **sunfish**. Sunfish are pancake-shaped fish that look like they've been sandwiched between two walls. These funny fish are huge, and can weigh almost as much as a car! Keen-eyed Little Explorers might spot one sunbathing on the ocean's surface.

The open ocean is home to fish that humans like to eat, such as **tuna**, **salmon** and **mackerel**. Humans eat a lot of fish, but catching *too many* fish can be bad for the ocean. This is because the ecosystem requires **balance** to thrive.

Careful fishing practices mean we make sure to leave plenty of food for ocean predators – including mammals like **seals** and **dolphins**, larger fish like **sailfish** and, of course, **sharks**.

MIGRATION

Lots of animals cross the wide expanse of the open ocean every year, moving from the cold and food-rich water to warmer areas where they have their babies. This movement is called **migration**.

Every year, patient Big and Little Explorers expedition to lookouts along the coast to try to spot migrating whales.

Other animals migrate too. **Leatherback sea turtles** travel some of the **longest** distances of any animal on Earth – covering thousands of kilometres all the way from Indonesia to Alaska.

The **cownose stingray** migration is one of the most spectacular sights on Earth as these graceful stingrays migrate in swarms of more than **ten thousand** dancing creatures.

DID YOU KNOW?

A group of stingrays is called a fever.

THE KRAKEN

There are many stories that have been told to explain the mysteries of the open ocean.

Old Norse sagas tell the legend of the **kraken**. Thought to be a giant, tentacled creature, the kraken was regularly blamed for seizing ships and eating them. Big Explorers thought that this was just superstition until they discovered the existence of the **giant squid**.

People searched for the giant squid for a long time, but they couldn't find any alive until recently.

The giant squid
is a very shy
creature that lives
quite deep in the ocean,
which is why it took until
the 21st century for anyone
to find one to photograph and study.

Even now, there's a lot we don't know about
these animals.

Big Explorers don't think the giant squid is the
kraken of old Norse tales, but it's very possible
that this huge, strange-looking creature
inspired the legend.

OPEN OCEAN

Okay, Little Explorers, let's dive deep, deep, deep down to the midnight zone and the ocean floor.

Welcome to the **DEEP OCEAN**.

DEEP OCEAN

51

The midnight zone starts **1000 metres** below the ocean's surface. Big Explorers have discovered that the midnight zone accounts for more than **half** of Earth's ocean.

That means there's a lot for Little Explorers to discover!

No sun can reach the ocean's depths. This is because sunlight is absorbed and scattered as it travels through water. After 1000 metres, there's not a lot of light left!

Without sunlight, there's also not a lot of warmth – in fact, the water of the deep ocean is nearly freezing. Brrr! Without light or warmth, a lot of the ocean life we've learnt about so far is unable to survive.

It's not completely dark in the deep ocean though. There might not be sunlight, but there are millions of tiny pinpricks of light from animals and microorganisms.

LIVING LIGHT

While humans rely on things like fire or electricity to create light, some creatures can create their own!

We call this bioluminescence.

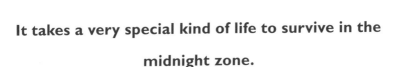

It takes a very special kind of life to survive in the midnight zone.

CREATURES OF THE DEEP

The waters of the midnight zone are filled with some of the **strangest** animals on Earth.

Because food is scarce in the deep ocean, predators that live here often have huge mouths filled with very large teeth to make sure they can eat anything they find.

They have also adapted clever ways of catching prey.

Angler fish can open their mouths large enough to swallow prey almost twice their size. They also take advantage of **bioluminescence** by using a lure on their heads. This lure mimics the light of smaller creatures.

Angler fish aren't the only fish that produce light in the deep ocean. **Vampire squid** expel a cloud of bioluminescent particles when they're threatened. These particles confuse predators so the vampire squid can escape.

Unlike their name suggests, vampire squid aren't actually predators themselves. Instead, they are **scavengers** and **opportunistic hunters** that primarily feed on little particles of food that fall through the water from the open ocean above.

Brittle sea stars, which are related to starfish, are also scavengers. They use their long spindly legs to crawl from place to place.

SEAMOUNTS

The deep ocean also includes the **ocean floor**. Just like on land, the terrain down here is home to mountains, canyons and volcanoes amid the vast expanse of rock and sand.

In fact, the ocean floor is home to some of the biggest mountains on Earth! These are called **seamounts**, and they are teeming with life.

Some seamounts are home to lifeforms that can only be found on that particular seamount. These species thrive in the nutrient-rich water that is pushed up the side of the mountains by deep-ocean currents.

Seamounts are often covered in **sea anemones, sponges, sea fans** and even **deep-sea coral,** all of which provide homes for animals like **starfish, worms** and **lobsters.**

It is estimated that Earth's oceans contain more than 31,000 seamounts. That's a lot of underwater mountains to explore!

HYDROTHERMAL VENTS

Hydrothermal vents are underwater cracks in the surface of the Earth that erupt with hot water and gas.

The waters around a hydrothermal vent are **warm** and full of **nutrients** that allow the plants and animals that live there to survive without sunlight.

In fact, there is so much life around hydrothermal vents that scientists are continually discovering creatures that are specially **adapted** to this hot water.

The kinds of life that thrive in this extreme environment are called extremophiles.

The animals down here are very different to other sea creatures. There are **shrimp** without eyes; and giant **tube worms** that grow up to 3 metres long and live in large colonies clustered together like seaweed. There are even some creatures that have adapted to survive in environments from the boiling waters of vents and the freezing waters of the deep ocean, all the way up to the sunlight zone, like the **Japanese spider crab**.

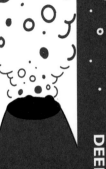

CHALLENGER DEEP

The **very, very, very** deepest part of the ocean is called **Challenger Deep**. The ocean floor here is almost 11 kilometres below the water's surface! It is part of the **Mariana Trench**, which is a long chasm in the ocean floor between Papua New Guinea and Japan.

Unlike seamounts and hydrothermal vents, there is very little life to be found in the Mariana Trench.

This is because the waters of the trench aren't fed nutrients from ocean currents like the waters around seamounts, or through the Earth's crust like hydrothermal vents.

Exploring the **deep ocean** can tell us a lot about life on the surface. Big Scientists use research gathered from these waters to tell them more about earthquakes and tsunamis, how we might improve our medicine, suggest new ways for us to use energy and help show us how we can best protect our natural world.

THE ATLANTIS MYTH

The legend of **Atlantis** has been around for a long, long time.

Thousands of years ago, an ancient Greek writer named **Plato** wrote a story about a city called Atlantis, that was supposed to have existed thousands of years before he was alive.

He wrote about a paradise of lush islands which were home to people who lived in houses decorated with gold and precious gems. But then earthquakes and a massive flood saw Atlantis and its treasures sink into the ocean, never to be seen again.

There have been many theories on where Atlantis might be found. Somewhere around Europe is one of the most popular guesses, while other people think the city could have existed near Indonesia, in the Carribbean or even near Antarctica.

No one has found Atlantis yet, and the majority of Big Explorers agree that, since we've mapped out most of the ocean floor, the legend is just a myth. But until we know everything about the ocean, it's impossible to say for sure ...

We've explored coastal waters, the open ocean and the deep ocean, but there's one last, very special part of the ocean we haven't yet discovered.

Little Explorers, it's time to dive into **POLAR WATERS**.

The oceans at the very top and bottom of our planet are different to the water that covers the rest of the Earth.

Big Explorers describe the Arctic and Southern oceans as POLAR WATERS.

These oceans at Earth's poles are terribly cold. Frigid air temperatures, especially in winter, cause the polar oceans' surfaces to freeze. This **sea ice** is constantly shifting and breaking apart. In winter, polar waters sit beneath an endless night, seeing barely any sunlight until the seasons begin to change.

These conditions make our polar oceans some of the **harshest** environments on Earth. But life here is uniquely adapted to thrive and the waters are full of nutrients.

But the two polar oceans are not the same! The **ARCTIC OCEAN** at the North Pole is home to animals like **polar bears, narwhals, beluga whales** and **walruses.**

The water surrounding Antarctica is the **SOUTHERN OCEAN**. Antarctica is actually a desert! It is so cold and dry that no animals that exist purely on land can live there. Like the Arctic Ocean, the Southern Ocean is home to **whales** and **seals,** but the waters of the South Pole are also home to something the north doesn't have – **penguins!**

These polar oceans are home to a variety of marine life, some of which is found at the North *and* South poles!

No matter whether it's the Arctic or Southern Ocean, or any of the oceans in between, all of Earth's marine waters are home to **krill** and **plankton**. These tiny plants and animals are a very important part of the ocean's **food web**.

Some of the larger animals in the ocean's food web are **orcas**, or killer whales. Actually the world's largest dolphin, orcas hunt fish and seals all over the globe.

Elephant seals, with their rather large noses, can be found in the waters of both polar oceans, but nowhere in between.

Other ocean animals migrate between the poles and warmer waters, depending on whether it's the right time of year to eat or breed. **Humpback whales** return to the cold polar oceans every summer to find rich feeding grounds.

Arctic terns also migrate, flying all the way from the *North* Pole to the *South* Pole, following the warmer weather.

THE SOUTHERN OCEAN

There are many animals unique to the Southern Ocean, but the one most Little Explorers think of first is the **penguin**.

Almost all penguins live in the southern hemisphere. Those who live in the Southern Ocean make their homes on the continent of Antarctica and the islands that surround it.

The biggest penguin in the Southern Ocean is the **emperor penguin,** which is as tall as a six-year-old human! Emperor penguins live on the ice, huddling together to protect themselves against the wind.

Lots of other penguins, like **Adélie penguins** and **gentoo penguins,** live here too.

The Southern Ocean is also home to a lot of seals! **Weddell seals** are not found in any other ocean. They hunt

fish, squid and octopus and can hold their breath for 45 minutes. Because Weddell seals hunt under the ice, they use their teeth to cut air holes when they need to breathe.

Leopard seals are the greatest predators in these waters. Most leopard seals hunt penguins and the babies of other kinds of seal, but they'll eat almost anything they can catch.

THE ARCTIC OCEAN

The Arctic Ocean is the world's smallest ocean, and much of its life exists under a thick layer of ice.

Polar bears are one of the most well-known arctic animals. Though polar bears look white, their skin is actually black! This helps them soak up all of the sun's warmth. Their thick fur is much lighter though, and it helps them blend into the ice and snow. Polar bears also have a thick layer of fat which insulates them against the freezing arctic temperatures. They usually hunt on the sea ice, sneaking up on seals or keeping watch over their breathing holes. They can smell their prey even if it's beneath a metre of snow and ice. Now that's a powerful nose!

Walruses live on the ice and hunt in the water too. Closely related to seals and sea lions, walruses are known for their long tusks. They are also huge and can weigh more than a car!

The Arctic Ocean is home to some very special types of whale. **Bowhead whales, belugas** and **narwhals** all live in the waters around the North Pole, relying on the sea ice to provide both homes for their food and protection. The bowhead whale has the biggest mouth of any whale, and belugas sing together and mimic other sounds.

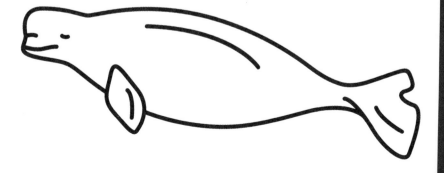

NARWHALS

Narwhals are whales with a long, spiralled tooth that protrudes from their mouth like a tusk. They're very, very shy, which means that humans don't see them very often.

The **Inuit**, who live by the Arctic Ocean, tell a legend that says the narwhal's horn was formed from the hair of a woman who fell off a hunting ship.

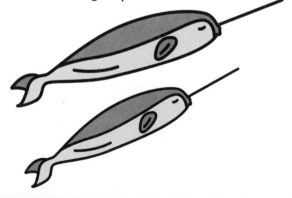

The people of medieval Europe called narwhals the **unicorns of the sea**. People thought that a narwhal's spiralled tusk had magical powers, and they would pay Vikings and other traders from the North Pole a lot of gold to be able to have a narwhal tusk of their own.

The tusk of a male narwhal can grow up to three metres long. But Big Scientists are pretty sure they're not magic.

No one really knows what a narwhal uses its tusk for though.

What do you think it could be for?

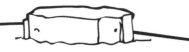

ALL ABOUT ICE

The ice in our polar waters has a huge impact on our climate.

Both the Arctic Ocean and Southern Ocean are home to **permanent ice** – this means that part of the ocean's surface is frozen all year round. As our world warms, more of this permanent ice is melting during summer, and less sea ice is forming during winter.

Lighter colours, like ice, reflect the sun and its heat, while darker colours, like the surface of the ocean, absorb it.

The more ice we have in the Arctic and Southern Oceans, the more heat from the sun is reflected away from Earth.

This **slows down** the rise of our global temperature over time.

Thankfully, Big and Little Explorers have already taken steps to protect the ice in our polar waters.

An important part of our atmosphere, known as the **ozone layer**, protects us from the sun. We have started to shrink the hole in this layer, which means our climate isn't changing as quickly as it was before, so we have a little bit more time to fix it!

A lot of people think the ice at the poles is *just* frozen water, but we Little Explorers know better!

> Our polar oceans are littered with sea ice and icebergs. Sea ice is formed from salty ocean water, but icebergs are formed from fresh water, and are actually considered 'land ice'. This is because icebergs are parts of glaciers that have broken off.

We often think of ice as white but, if you look closely, you can see the icebergs in our polar oceans are actually a **turquoise blue**. As snow falls on a glacier, it **compresses** the layers of freezing water underneath.

This pushes out the air bubbles and leaves beautiful, clear blue ice. The older ice is, the bluer it can be – if you see a very, very blue iceberg, it's likely to be very, very old!

Some ice in Antarctica is even **green!** At first, Big Scientists thought this was because there was a lot of **organic matter** – that is, things that were alive – trapped in the ice. Now, they think that the green colour might mean that there's a lot of the mineral **iron** in the ice.

Iron is a super important nutrient for plankton – which we know is one of the most important parts of the ocean's food web. If the green icebergs are full of iron, then they might be helping all life in the ocean to flourish.

MORE
TO
EXPLORE

There's a lot we don't know about the ocean.

In fact, Big Explorers estimate that we've only uncovered about **five per cent** of the things the ocean has to show us.

This is very exciting because it means that there is so much more that Big and Little Explorers can discover!

OCEAN EXPLORERS

There are many different jobs done by Big Explorers that help us to learn more about our oceans.

Oceanography is the name of the science that studies the ocean. There are four different types of oceanographers.

Marine biologists study the plants and animals that live in the ocean, by looking at the different ecosystems and all the lifeforms that make the ocean their home.

Marine chemists study seawater and how it interacts with things like air and pollution.

Marine geologists study the ocean floor and look at underwater structures like seamounts. They also study underwater volcanoes!

Physical oceanographers study things like waves and the tides, and how coastlines were formed.

Some ocean explorers are **carers,** who help to look after marine life when it becomes sick or injured. And there are those who help keep track of when and where they see marine creatures, like migrating whales.

Artists and writers can be ocean explorers too!

By creating photographs, films, books, articles and more, these ocean explorers share many of the amazing things that can be discovered in our ocean with those who can't visit it.

HOW TO EXPLORE

There are lots of ways for Little Explorers to discover more about the ocean.

The best way to explore the ocean is to visit it. Ask a Big Explorer to wander with you along the shoreline of a **beach,** or to scramble carefully over rocks at low tide to peer into **rock pools.** Perhaps you might even be able to go snorkelling over a **coral reef** or **kelp forest!** You can look for whales during migration season too.

Sometimes, ocean creatures are brought to places called **aquariums**, where Little Explorers can see them up close!

THE OCEAN

Visiting the ocean isn't the only way to discover what lies under the waves. Little Explorers can watch documentaries or read books about all the wonderful things that live in the ocean. Your teacher or librarian can help you learn more!

HELPING OUR OCEAN

Our ocean is so very important.

We know it's full of life, and that it's one of
the last great wildernesses on Earth.

Our waters and everything that goes on inside
them affect Earth's climate.

**As Little Explorers, one of our most
important missions is to protect
our oceans.**

EXPLORING WITH CARE

We should always make sure that we observe what we find without disturbing it — which means we need to look, but not touch!

Touching the creatures we see can injure them, or scare them away from the places they rely on for food and protection. We can sometimes even scare parents away from their babies.

It's also important that we don't remove anything that makes up an ecosystem, like shells or rocks, because these provide homes and shelter for many animals.

RUBBISH

But there is one thing that us Little Explorers *should* remove from ocean environments when we see it: **rubbish**.

Rubbish is one of the most dangerous things in our oceans.

Some animals eat rubbish, which can cause problems with their insides. Some animals get trapped in rubbish, and can't swim or eat properly.

Doing what we can to ensure the ocean stays full of life is the responsibility of every Little Explorer.

There are **five** oceans on our planet, and a lot of seas.

Seas are usually **smaller** and **shallower** than oceans.

The ocean covers a lot of our planet's surface, and contains most of Earth's **water** supply.

It's very important to **protect** the ocean as much as we can.

The water of the ocean is divided into three zones, depending on how much sunlight penetrates the water. These are the **sunlight zone**, the **twilight zone** and the **midnight zone**.

The ocean contains the most life out of all the ecosystems on our planet.

This means it has a lot of **biodiversity!**

GLOSSARY

BIODIVERSITY: the variety of living things and ecosystems.

BIOLUMINESCENCE: light that is created by living things.

COAST: where the ocean meets the land.

CONTINENT: one of Earth's main land masses.

CURRENTS: ribbons of fast-moving water.

ECOSYSTEM: a community of living things, and the environment they live in.

ENDANGERED: when a living thing is so rare that it's in danger of not existing anymore.

ENVIRONMENT: all the things that make up an object, plant or creature's surroundings.

EXPLORER: a curious person who examines the world around them, or seeks to discover new things.

FISH: a type of animal that lives in the water.

GLACIER: a river of ice on land that moves very slowly and accumulates over many decades.

MAMMAL: a type of animal that feeds its babies milk.

MARINE RESERVE: a place where the ocean environment is protected.

MICROORGANISM: a very, very, very small living thing.

OCEANOGRAPHY: the science of studying the ocean.

PHYTOPLANKTON: plankton that are plants.

POLE: the point at the very top or bottom of our planet.

TIDE: the rise and fall of the ocean, seen most dramatically in coastal waters.

ZONES: the word we use to refer to the layers of the ocean.

ZOOPLANKTON: plankton that are animals.

PUFFIN
QUIZ

1. What animal loves to play in **kelp forests?**

2. What animal do Big Explorers think inspired the **kraken** myth?

3. What **zone** is the deepest part of the ocean?

4. At which pole can you find **polar bears?**

5. What colour is the ice in very old **glaciers?**

ANSWERS:
1. seals 2. the giant squid 3. the midnight zone 4. the North Pole 5. blue.

A PUFFIN LITTLE BOOK